SPACE MYSTERIES

COULD WE LIVE ON OTHER PLANETS?

Gareth Stevens
Publishing

BY MICHAEL PORTMAN

Please visit our website, www.garethstevens.com. For a free color catalog of all our high-quality books, call toll free 1-800-542-2595 or fax 1-877-542-2596.

Library of Congress Cataloging-in-Publication Data

Portman, Michael
Could we live on other planets / Michael Portman.
    p. cm. — (Space mysteries)
Includes index.
ISBN 978-1-4339-9214-8 (pbk.)
ISBN 978-1-4339-9215-5 (6-pack)
ISBN 978-1-4339-9213-1 (library binding)
1. Space astronomy — Miscellanea — Juvenile literature. 2. Space astronomy 3. Planets — Juvenile literature. I. Title
QB602.P853 2014
523.4—d23

First Edition

Published in 2014 by
Gareth Stevens Publishing
111 East 14th Street, Suite 349
New York, NY 10003

Copyright © 2014 Gareth Stevens Publishing

Designer: Katelyn E. Reynolds
Editor: Therese Shea

Photo credits: Cover, pp. 1, 23 Steven Hobbs/Stocktrek Images/Getty Images; cover, pp. 1, 3–32 (background texture) David M. Schrader/Shutterstock.com; pp. 3–32 (fun fact graphic) © iStockphoto.com/spxChrome; pp. 5, 9 iStockphoto/Thinkstock.com; p. 6 Hemera/Thinkstock.com; pp. 7, 11, 13 NASA; p. 10 Comstock/Thinkstock.com; p. 12 Ralph Morse/Time & Life Pictures/Getty Images; p. 15 (top) NASA/JPL; p. 15 (bottom) NASA/JSC; p. 17 NASA/Ames/JPL-Caltech; p. 19 Ittiz/Wikipedia.com; p. 21 NASA Ames Research Center; p. 25 NASA/JPL-Caltech; p. 27 Michael Dunning/Photographer's Choice/Getty Images; p. 29 © Mark A. Garlick / space-art.co.uk.

Printed in the United States of America

CPSIA compliance information: Batch #CS13GS: For further information contact Gareth Stevens, New York, New York at 1-800-542-2595.

CONTENTS

Words in the glossary appear in **bold** type the first time they are used in the text.

HOME AWAY FROM EARTH

Have you ever looked at the sky on a starry night and wondered what it would be like to live on another planet? Scientists think the universe contains billions of planets. So far, we've only discovered a fraction. Is it possible that we could live on any of them?

It's important to know what makes Earth an ideal place for life. Earth is located in an area of our **solar system** called the **habitable** zone. It's neither too hot nor too cold for liquid water to exist.

OUT OF THIS WORLD!

Scientists have nicknamed the habitable zone the Goldilocks zone, after the children's fairy tale.

Is a new home planet somewhere out there?

5

WATER WORLD

Water is necessary for life on Earth. As far as we know, water is needed for life on other planets, too. Without liquid water, the **chemical** reactions of life couldn't take place. If people are to live on other planets, liquid water must be present.

Some plants and animals can stay alive, or survive, for long periods of time without water. People can only last about a week. That's why finding a planet in the habitable zone is so important.

Seventy percent of Earth is covered with water.

Earth is sometimes called the "blue planet." Seen from space, it's mostly blue because of the oceans.

JUST BREATHE

Earth is surrounded by a thick mix of gases called the atmosphere. Earth's atmosphere is made mostly of nitrogen and oxygen. Our atmosphere is what allows us to breathe. For people to live on the surface of another planet, the planet must have an atmosphere very similar to Earth's.

Earth also has a **magnetic field** that guards us from harmful solar **radiation**. Without that magnetic field, life on the surface of Earth would be almost impossible.

OUT OF THIS WORLD!

Earth's atmosphere keeps temperatures from becoming too hot or too cold from day to night.

Any planet that we might want to live on would need an Earthlike atmosphere and magnetic field.

9

CHANGING LIFE

Life on Earth has had over 4.5 billion years to change to fit the conditions of our planet. The plants and animals able to survive in different **environments** on Earth might have a harder time surviving more extreme environments on another planet.

Many animals, including people, have a body temperature of around 98.6°F (37°C). Changes in body temperature of just a few degrees hotter or colder can be deadly. Any planet we hope to **colonize** will need to have temperatures similar to those on Earth.

Life on Earth exists even in the harshest conditions. Conditions are even harsher on other planets, though.

GRAVITY

Life on Earth has also grown to suit our planet's **gravity**. On a smaller planet with less gravity, we would weigh less and our muscles would shrink. We'd also have a very hard time keeping our feet on the ground! This is why the astronauts who landed on the moon wore very heavy spacesuits that made it easier for them to walk.

On the other hand, if a planet were bigger than Earth and its gravity stronger, we wouldn't be able to move!

astronauts weightless in space

If you weighed 60 pounds (27 kg) on Earth, you'd weigh 10 pounds (4.5 kg) on the moon!

LIFE ON MARS?

Mars is the most Earthlike planet in the solar system. Some scientists think Mars is the best possibility in our solar system for human colonization. It has minerals, such as iron, that could be mined and used for the construction of buildings. Plus, it's not too far away.

Mars also contains ice that could be melted to provide water. In fact, many places on Mars look a lot like Earth. However, looks can be misleading.

OUT OF THIS WORLD!

The atmosphere of Mars is made mostly of carbon dioxide. Carbon dioxide is what people breathe out.

Photos sent back from Mars (top) show a landscape similar to some areas of Earth (bottom).

CHALLENGES

Mars lies on the outer edge of the habitable zone. It's too cold for liquid water, and its atmosphere is unable to support life as far as we know. But Mars is very similar to what Earth was like billions of years ago.

When Earth first formed, it had no oxygen. Then **bacteria** grew, producing oxygen that slowly entered the atmosphere. This allowed larger plants and animals to grow. Perhaps the same process that made Earth's atmosphere breathable could be repeated on Mars.

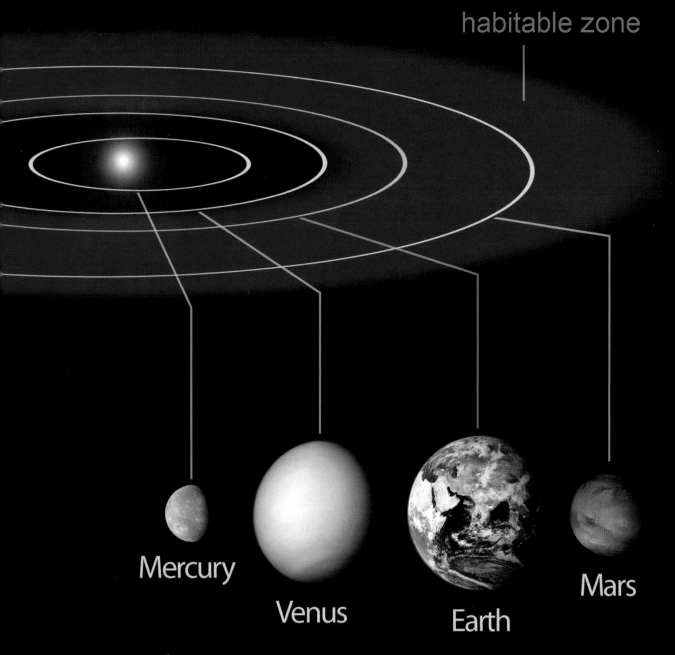

habitable zone

Mercury

Venus

Earth

Mars

17

TERRAFORMING

If a planet lies in the habitable zone but isn't able to support life, it may be possible to change the planet. This process is called terraforming. Terraforming a planet such as Mars would include heating it up somehow.

Possibly, giant mirrors could be placed in **orbit** around a planet to direct sunlight to heat the polar ice caps. By melting polar ice caps, enough carbon dioxide might be **released** to create an atmosphere thick enough to trap heat.

OUT OF THIS WORLD!

Comets are made of ice and dust. If a planet doesn't have water, it might be possible to crash an icy comet into it.

Terraforming is just an idea right now. Will scientists try to terraform
Mars in the future? Here's an artist's idea of a terraformed Mars.

GROWING LIFE

Once the planet is warm enough, liquid water can flow. Bacteria and other small organisms can then be introduced. These tiny life-forms would prepare the surface for larger plants and trees. Plants and trees take in carbon dioxide and release oxygen.

After enough time, the planet could have a breathable atmosphere. However, this huge project might take thousands of years to complete. Right now, scientists are decades away from even beginning to terraform a planet such as Mars.

OUT OF THIS WORLD!
Too little or too much oxygen is deadly to people.

Making a planet habitable for life could take hundreds, thousands, or even hundreds of thousands of years. After all, it took millions of years for Earth to be able to support life.

ARTIFICIAL STRUCTURES

We already know that it's possible for people to survive in space for extended periods of time. The International Space Station (ISS) orbits Earth about 220 miles (354 km) above the surface.

Currently, the most realistic method for planetary colonization is to build structures on or below a planet's surface. The planet must have resources to maintain these structures. Continually transporting supplies would be expensive and time consuming. Large structures called biodomes could provide an **artificial** environment that would keep people safe from a harmful atmosphere.

OUT OF THIS WORLD!

The ISS has been continually occupied since November 2, 2000. More than 200 people have visited it.

Ideally, we would find a planet so similar to Earth that it's ready to support us. But if not, artificial environments might be a solution until the planet is terraformed.

GETTING THERE

Mars is one of our closest neighbors, but it would still be a huge challenge to send people to visit its surface. A trip from Earth to Mars takes between 150 and 300 days. Because of the large amount of fuel necessary for the round-trip, a mission to Mars would be very expensive.

Sending enough supplies to actually live on Mars would be an even greater challenge. Naturally, if more people were to live on Mars, more supplies would be needed.

OUT OF THIS WORLD!

The longest anyone has ever spent in space was 438 days. A Russian astronaut lived aboard a space station from January 1994 to March 1995.

Scientists are trying to build spacecraft that could fly to Mars more quickly.

25

WHY MOVE?

It might be hard to imagine, but time is running out for planet Earth. Scientists believe that in roughly 2 billion years, our sun will burn so hot that the oceans will boil away. Before that happens, it's possible that a large space rock, such as an asteroid or comet, will hit Earth. It could cause great harm.

But perhaps Earth will simply become too crowded to support a growing population. Some scientists think it may be necessary to find a new planet because we're using up Earth's resources.

Large asteroids and comets have hit Earth in the past.
This was likely the cause of the dinosaurs dying out.

27

IN THE FUTURE

Billions of stars exist outside our solar system. Planets orbit many of them. Scientists are searching for planets that lie within the habitable zone of their star. The Kepler space telescope built by NASA (National Aeronautics and Space Administration) searches for Earthlike planets within the habitable zone.

However, even if Kepler finds a planet that could support life, getting there will be the greatest challenge of all. The journey will certainly be tough, but it may be possible one day.

OUT OF THIS WORLD!

So far, the Kepler space telescope has discovered 105 planets outside our solar system.

FUTURE COLONIZATION METHODS

terraforming	artificial environments
transforming a planet to suit our needs	creating buildings that could support life

This Saturn-size planet, Kepler-35b, orbits two suns!

GLOSSARY

artificial: made by people and not by nature

bacteria: tiny creatures that can only be seen with a microscope

challenge: a test of abilities

chemical: matter that can be mixed with other matter to cause changes

colonize: to establish a colony

environment: the conditions that surround a living thing and affect the way it lives

gravity: the force that pulls objects toward the center of a planet or star

habitable: suitable for life

magnetic field: the area around a magnetic body where its pull is felt

orbit: to travel in a circle or oval around something, or the path used to make that trip

radiation: waves of energy

release: to let go

solar system: the sun and all the space objects that orbit it, including the planets and their moons

FOR MORE INFORMATION

BOOKS

O'Brien, Patrick. *You Are the First Kid on Mars.* New York, NY: Putnam's Sons, 2009.

Solway, Andrew. *Can We Travel to the Stars? Space Flight and Space Exploration.* Chicago, IL: Heinemann Library, 2006.

WEBSITES

Fun with Astronomy
www.kidsastronomy.com
Play games, watch videos, and learn about space.

How Terraforming Mars Will Work
science.howstuffworks.com/terraforming2.htm
Read about the different ways some people think Mars could be made habitable for people.

Kepler: A Search for Habitable Planets
www.nasa.gov/mission_pages/kepler/main/index.html
Read about the ongoing Kepler mission.

INDEX